Original title:
Under the Christmas Moon

Copyright © 2024 Creative Arts Management OÜ
All rights reserved.

Author: Colin Harrington
ISBN HARDBACK: 978-9916-90-896-9
ISBN PAPERBACK: 978-9916-90-897-6

Enchanted Pines Adorned in Light

The pines wear gowns of twinkling cheer,
With squirrels reenacting a wild frontier.
The ornaments dangle, a sight quite bizarre,
As daddy gets stuck in the starry tar.

Snowflakes are giggling, they flirt and tease,
While rabbits dance clumsily in the freeze.
An elf trips over a candy cane,
Chasing his hat, shouting all the more insane.

The Magic We Breathe in the Stillness

Cocoa's steaming, marshmallows leap,
While giggling kids play hide and peep.
The cookies have vanished, oh what a fright,
I swear it was Santa, sneaking out of sight.

Gifts wrapped with bows, some oddly shaped,
A knitted sweater that really escaped.
Laughter rings out, oh what a night,
Who put the cat in the holiday lights?

Frostbitten Whispers of Love

A snowman stands, quite proud and round,
With a carrot nose stuck awkwardly down.
His scarf's slid right over one beady eye,
As the kids giggle and ask, 'Why oh why?'

Jingle bells jangle with a comical sound,
As Grandma attempts to dance all around.
Her moves are quite catchy, a sight to behold,
While grandpa just chuckles, too tired and old.

A Wish on Midnight's Breath

A wish is made, on frosty breath,
For a toy train from the North, oh what a quest!
But instead in the morning, what did I find?
A pair of bright socks, mismatched and blind.

The night was filled with snickers and snorts,
As cookies became reindeer snack reports.
Hoping for magic, we waited so late,
Only to see Dad eating our plate!

Embracing Midnight's Glow

Santa's sleigh took a wild dive,
Rudolph shouted, 'We're alive!'
Elves are spinning in delight,
Hot cocoa's splashed—what a sight!

Snowmen dance with silly grace,
Frosty boots play a funny chase.
Laughter echoes through the night,
As snowballs fly with pure delight.

A Celestial Winter Serenade

The stars are tickling the sky,
While penguins waddle and sigh.
A jingle bell starts to play,
As polar bears join the ballet.

A snowflake lands on a cat,
Paws go swiping—imagine that!
Squirrels plan a grand parade,
On ice, they slip but never fade.

Silent Prayers Beneath Starlit Dreams

Whispers ride the frosty breeze,
Snowflakes fall with playful tease.
The tree's all dressed in glimmering light,
While cookies vanish out of sight.

A reindeer practices his snort,
Joining in a snowball sport.
The moon giggles, watching near,
As carolers down the street cheer!

Frosted Echoes of Yule

Tinsel glitters like a prank,
As cats perform a daring plank.
Chill vibes wrap around the day,
While mischief dances in the hay.

The fireplace groans in a fit,
While soggy mittens take a sit.
Under blankets, kittens fight,
For a place in the warm, soft light.

Candlelit Dreams Amidst Winter's Chill

In a cabin so cozy and bright,
The snowmen all started a fight.
With carrots for noses, oh dear!
They danced with a elf, filled with cheer.

The candles were flickering fast,
While gingerbread men ran and amassed.
They baked up a scheme, full of glee,
To eat all the sweets and then flee!

The Magic of Nighttime Wonder

On rooftops, the reindeer make noise,
While Santa just plays with his toys.
He tripped on the sleigh, oh what a sight,
And tangled the string lights so tight!

The stars in the sky wink and blink,
As hot cocoa spills down the sink.
The marshmallows float like a dream,
While the cat plots to steal all the cream.

Boughs of Evergreen Under Starry Skies

The tree stood tall, with ornaments placed,
Yet the cat made sure they were displaced.
With tinsel in tow and a jump so spry,
That sneaky little kitty flew high!

Elves scampered 'round with cookies in hand,
But one took a dive in the flour stand.
With powdered sugar, they giggled in jest,
A snowy surprise in their festive quest!

Silvered Silence Among the Pines

Amidst the pines, it's a laugh-filled scene,
Where squirrels wear hats just like a queen.
They nibble on nuts, so boldly, with pride,
While the snowmen are caught in a slide!

The lights twinkle bright, with joy and with cheer,
As snowflakes do twirl, swooping near.
A laughter erupts from the frosty night,
In this whimsical world, everything feels right!

Celestial Reflections on a Silent Eve

Snowflakes dance like silly sprites,
The neighbors' lights are blinding brights.
My cat thinks she's a reindeer queen,
Chasing shadows, she's quite the scene.

The stars giggle, twinkling loud,
As we hum tunes, feeling proud.
Hot cocoa spills like joyful cheer,
While I hunt for my missing ear.

Echoes of Laughter in the Snow

Snowmen sporting mismatched hats,
My dog chases, oh look, more bats!
Sledding down on a cardboard base,
Wishing I'd packed some extra grace.

The chilly air brings silly fright,
When I slip, it's a comical sight.
Laughter echoes, breaking the chill,
As we tumble and roll down the hill.

Gleaming Ornaments and Whispered Secrets

Tangled lights, an ornament war,
Who knew holiday prep could bore?
A cat on the tree, what a sight,
Wrapping paper flies left and right.

Grandma's cookies, a rock-hard treat,
Might need tools for a proper feat.
We laugh, debate, is it a pie?
Or a doorstop that's gone awry?

Beneath the Icy Canopy of Night

Icicles hang like a frozen choir,
The snowmen melt, or maybe retire.
What's that noise? Is it a ghost?
Nope, just Uncle Fred, that's the most!

Joyful chaos fills the air bright,
While we bicker over the next bite.
In our hats, we look quite absurd,
But who cares? Laughter's the best word!

Nordic Nights Sparkling with Wonder

Snowflakes dance like tiny stars,
Elves are juggling candy bars.
Reindeer play games in the snow,
While Santa's stuck in a sleigh dough.

Frosty breath makes quite the scene,
A snowman's sporting shades of green.
Mittens lost, they start to roam,
And sing carols back to their home.

A Hearth's Warm Embrace

Crackling logs, they laugh a lot,
As the cat steals the best warm spot.
A marshmallow fight breaks out near,
With cocoa splashed on everyone here.

Shadows dance like silly fools,
While Grandma remarks on our 'cool' rules.
Jingle bells ring by mistake,
And cousin Fred makes the cake shake.

Illuminated Wishes in the Chill

Twinkling lights all tangled up tight,
Uncle Joe swears he'll get them right.
The tree leans a bit to the side,
And the ornaments start a joyride.

Everyone's dressed in holiday flair,
A poodle dons a festive pair.
Socks with holes are now the trend,
As we giggle and all pretend.

Stories Told by the Fire's Glow

Gather 'round, it's tale time fast,
Uncle's jokes are a legendary blast.
Grandpa shares tales of yesteryear,
With a wink, he claims he's a deer.

The fire crackles with a cheeky grin,
As Grandma whispers, "Where have you been?"
We chuckle and sip our spiced cheer,
Wishing more nights would last all year.

Shadows Dance on Snow

Snowmen wobble, hats askew,
Snowballs fly, yells ensue!
Squirrels slide with glee and flair,
While reindeer dance, tails in the air.

Footprints lead to nowhere fast,
A chase of laughter that can't last!
Frosty noses peek and grin,
As the moon laughs, let the fun begin!

Twinkling Lights and Frosty Breezes

Stringed lights dangle, what a sight,
They blink and twirl through the night!
Cats in hats, plotting schemes,
Of chasing shadows and silly dreams.

Frosty breath and chuckles rise,
As snowflakes fall like sweet surprise.
Neighbors peek, a light-hearted fuss,
Who's stealing cookies? Oh, that's us!

Echoes of Joy Beneath the Stars

Giggles echo, laughter so bright,
As snowmen wobble in pure delight.
Hot cocoa spills, oh what a mess,
But who can fret in such happiness?

Candy canes spark the winter air,
While pets wear sweaters, without a care.
Mittens fly in a silly race,
Stars twinkle, with a grin on their face!

The Night's Blanket of White

A blanket of white, soft and thick,
Gives way to snowball tricks that stick.
Children dash with squeals and cheers,
While sleds whiz by, powered by peers.

Snowflakes dance, a frosty spree,
While adults search for their lost key.
Hot toddies shared with laughter so clear,
As ice skaters glide to music we hear!

Embers of Memory in Winter's Embrace

Snowflakes dance like tiny stars,
Landing softly on my car.
I swear they're plotting with my cat,
To launch a snowball—how about that?

Hot cocoa spills, it stains my shirt,
The marshmallows act like they're alert.
A sip reveals a hidden thrill,
While puppies dash for every hill.

We drag our sleds with all our might,
And tumble down, what a delight!
A little kid screams with glee,
As snowflakes swirl all over me.

The evening wraps us in its glow,
As laughter sparkles, quite the show.
With cheeks so red, we raise a cheer,
Bring on the snow—let's crank the gear!

Starlit Vows Beneath Pine Canopies

In the woods where shadows play,
We mock the deer that skips away.
Tangled lights wrap round our legs,
These festive sprains need no peg!

We strung the bulbs without a thought,
But now they sparkle, oh what a lot!
A squirrel laughs at our tall dreams,
Snatching bulbs, as it seems.

Under branches, we can't get lost,
Giggles echo, at quite the cost.
A pie-baking contest in the breeze,
Flour flies like a winter sneeze.

We vow to keep this silly cheer,
As pine-scented laughter fills the air.
High-fives follow every mishap,
Our holiday spirit's a cozy clap!

Woven Dreams of Winter Nights

Wooly hats and mismatched mitts,
Racing snowmen, we throw our fits.
I made mine with carrot nose,
He looks like he's wearing a pose!

Skating on puddles that freeze like glass,
I tumble down, oh, what a pass!
Laughter erupts as I flop and roll,
The ice claims me, like a troll's role.

Our snowball fights turn fierce and wild,
With laughter ringing, every child.
But wait, who threw that? A snowball whips,
It hits my dad, and laughter rips!

By fireside we sip and scheme,
As shadows dance in winter's dream.
Oh, what fun in this chilly plight,
Tomorrow's snow will be just right!

Tinsel Tales in the Wooded Realm

In the woods where squirrels prance,
Tinsel hangs, they spin and dance.
One tries to dress a pine so tall,
But ends up stuck, oh what a fall!

Elves giggle from their secret nook,
Sharing stories, sneaky hooks.
A reindeer lost its way to cheer,
Now munches on a tree, oh dear!

Frosty hats on rabbits' heads,
Chasing shadows, weaving threads.
Twiggy wreaths in every place,
Just don't let them win the race!

The Heart's Glow in Winter's Embrace

In a blanket thick and white,
Snowmen wobble, quite a sight.
With a carrot nose and googly eyes,
They wear scarves made from old ties!

Chilly winds make noses bright,
But penguins join the frosty fight.
Sliding down the sledding hill,
With mugs of cocoa, hearts we thrill.

Jingle bells ring with a jolt,
While cats plot schemes to cause a revolt.
Decorations may hang askew,
As the dog steals a snack or two!

Celestial Paintings in the Sky

Stars wink brightly in the night,
Reindeer munching, what a sight.
Under the glow of twinkling lights,
They plan pranks to cause delights!

Santa's list gets lost, oh no,
In a snowball fight, they steal the show.
Rascally elves with sparkly flair,
Dodge snowflakes like they're made of air.

Lights turn on at every house,
Cats chase shadows as quick as a mouse.
Frosty drinks sit on a ledge,
While birds plot sweet holiday pledge!

Nightfall's Gift Wrapped in White

As dusk settles with a giggle,
The stars shine bright, ready to wiggle.
Gifts wrapped tight with ribbons galore,
But who knows what's in them? Just a chore!

A pickle ornament sits on a tree,
Laughter rings from each and every spree.
With glitter glued all over the floor,
The pet cat's now a sparkly bore!

With jokes and riddles shared around,
In this chill, laughter's the best sound.
For cozy nights and silly spats,
Bring on the fun, leave behind the spats!

The Lure of Starlit Frost

Snowflakes dance upon the street,
Kids throwing snowballs, not so neat.
Sleds zip by on tiresome trails,
Laughter echoes, winter prevails.

Hot cocoa spills, a marshmallow fight,
Twinkling lights make the world feel bright.
Some slip and slide, others just crawl,
Snowmen wobble, they might just fall!

Glittering Moments in Long Shadows

Shadows stretch beneath the trees,
Frosty whispers on the breeze.
Socks in mittens, quite the look,
Gingerbread houses, no one cooks!

Giggles travel through the night,
Unruly hounds chase after lights.
Cats on rooftops, stealing glances,
Chasing dreams in silly dances.

This Night of Wonder and Light

Elves on rooftops seem to sing,
While reindeers plot their silly fling.
Chimneys puff like stars in flight,
Laughter shines, oh what a sight!

Santa's list has snacks galore,
Cookies vanish; oh, what a score!
Cheerful jests, all hearts are bright,
In this magic, everything's right.

Frosty Dreams Beneath Shimmering Lights

Frosty noses, rosy cheeks,
Snowball fights, it's joy that speaks.
Dancing shadows, playful pranks,
Kids in mittens send their thanks.

Frosty whispers, stories spun,
Mittens missing, oh what fun!
Candles flicker, laughter flows,
In the air, pure magic grows.

Glistening Stars on a Frosty Night

The snowflakes dance, they whirl around,
A snowman snores upon the ground.
His carrot nose is far too large,
He dreams of sledding, quite the charge.

The stars above, they wink with glee,
As kids throw snowballs, wild and free.
A shivering cat, in a cozy hat,
Is plotting revenge on the cheeky brat.

Someone slipped on ice, oh what a sight,
They twirl like dancers, all in delight.
Hot cocoa spills, with marshmallows galore,
Laughter echoes, who could ask for more?

The night rolls on, with jokes to share,
Even grandma's dance is beyond compare.
With fuzzy socks and a holiday tune,
We smile and giggle, 'neath the silvery moon.

Embracing Spirits of the Season

The tree is up, all lopsided, oh dear,
Ornaments cling like they're full of cheer.
A cat climbs high, with a festive flair,
Then crashes down, without a care.

With mistletoe hanging, a nobody stalks,
Shouldering past in their fuzzy socks.
A chorus of giggles fills the air,
As someone leans in for a cheeky share.

The dance floor shimmies with holiday fun,
A twist here, a turn—oh look, he's run!
The punch bowl splashes, an icy mist,
Someone's hat flew off—what a twist!

Meanwhile, grandpa snores on the couch,
While kids debate who's the best grouch.
With bells that jingle, and hearts on fire,
We laugh the night away, never tire.

Charmed Moments Beneath Silent Skies

With cookies burning, a lovely scent,
A reindeer flies by, or so we pretend.
With kids all wrapped in a tangle of lights,
They giggle and tease under winter sights.

The snowman is dressed in dad's old coat,
But he looks quite dapper—give him a vote!
A squirrel in the yard, oh no, what a sight,
Is stealing our treats, with furry delight.

The carols are jumbled, notes go astray,
As uncle attempts to sing 'Jingle Bells' sway.
His dance moves are awkward, but full of cheer,
We join in, laughing at his holiday flair.

Time ticks on, with moments to seize,
The warmth of family, a gentle breeze.
A night full of snickers, under twinkling stars,
We'll cherish these memories, wherever we are.

The Luminescence of Quiet Gatherings

Gather 'round, let the stories fly,
Grandma shares tales, oh me, oh my!
With laughter bubbling like simmering stew,
The punch tastes great—not quite like glue.

A game of charades gets wild and loud,
Dad's secret move makes him so proud.
The dog joins in, with a wag and a bark,
While the lights dim low, it's now getting dark.

A rogue ornament rolls off the shelf,
And cousin Tim claims he did it himself.
With eggnog flowing and spirits bright,
We dance our way through this festive night.

And when we're done, it's time to share,
The love that fills each heart laid bare.
With smiles and jokes that cannot fade,
This merry gathering will never jade.

Frost-Embellished Wishes

A snowman in a scarf too bright,
He teeters left, then leans to the right.
With a carrot nose that just won't stay,
He sneezes flakes and shouts, "Hooray!"

Elves in boots with socks that mismatch,
Dancing 'round the yule-log hatch.
They trip on tinsel, squeal in delight,
Baking cookies late into the night.

Hushed Lullabies on Starlit Porches

Sipping cocoa, marshmallows float,
As a raccoon tries to steal a coat.
Santa's sleigh gets stuck in a tree,
While kids laugh wild with joyous glee.

A puppy in a hat that's way too tight,
Chases shadows until it's night.
With twinkling lights that blink and sway,
The carols drift and softly play.

The Glistening Pathway of Joy

Snowflakes pirouette on a bitter breeze,
As penguins ice-skate with the greatest of ease.
A cat in mittens gives it a try,
While pouncing and landing with a sigh.

Jingle bells ringing, chiming with cheer,
A squirrel's performance will cost you a beer.
Carrot sticks fly as laughter erupts,
In this festive chaos, no one interrupts.

Frosted Memories by the Firelight

Hot cider spills in a comical splash,
The cat leaps, it's a memorable clash.
Grandpa's snoring, but wait, what's that?
The wise old dog now wears his hat!

Gifts wrapped with tape too stubborn to peel,
Mistletoe hanging from the ceiling wheel.
With the flicker of flames, silliness grows,
As stories come alive with funny prose.

Romantic Embers in Winter's Scene

In the chilly air, a couple sneezes,
They laugh together, warming up with breezes.
Hot cocoa spills, a frothy delight,
As marshmallows float, oh, what a sight!

Frostbitten fingers, they cling so tight,
Trying to keep each other warm that night.
A snowman smiles, dressed up so formal,
While their snowball fight gets a bit too normal!

Laughter echoes through the snowy street,
As someone trips, oh what a feat!
They dance and twirl, just like a dream,
In the winter wonderland, a comical theme!

With rosy cheeks and noses aglow,
They share sweet secrets, giving love a show.
In this frosty world, love finds its place,
With giggles and grins, winter's warm embrace!

A Night Painted with Light

Twinkling lights hang, so festive and bright,
A clumsy elf stumbles, oh what a sight!
Tinsel gets tangled, amidst the cheer,
As everyone stops to lend a hand near.

Laughter resounds as ornaments fall,
The cat leaps up, oh what a brawl!
With stockings aglow, giggles erupt,
As cookie dough stains become a hiccup!

The tree sways gently, in rhythm and beat,
While grandpa snores softly, missing the treat.
Whispers of mischief float through the air,
And every heart lightens, joy everywhere!

With cheeky smiles and playful grins,
The night goes on as the fun begins.
In the glow of love, they share a toast,
To silly moments, that they love the most!

Snowfall's Gentle Murmur

Snowflakes tumble, a soft little dance,
While kids build a fort, taking a chance.
Snowballs are flying, laughter fills the air,
Until someone slips, oh, what a scare!

Wipe the snow off with an innocent grin,
As the friendly rivalry starts to begin.
Sledding down hills, like rockets they soar,
With hot cocoa breaks, they plead for more!

The dog joins in, chasing his tail,
While the mailman's lost beneath the white veil.
Frosty breath mingles with giggles galore,
As everyone gathers, knocking at doors!

In cozy homes, by the fire's warm glow,
They share tales of mischief, tales of woe.
With snowy scenes outside, pure skit and joy,
Winter's sense of humor exceeds every ploy!

Frosted Fables in the Stillness

The stars twinkle down, a frosty display,
As penguins in scarves march on their way.
Frosted stories intertwine in the night,
With giggles and tales that feel just right!

A bear sings off-key by the icy pond,
While the rabbits all cringe, and try to respond.
With a tap dance of snow, the moon giggles too,
Amidst all the clatter, of winter's debut!

Sledding adventures lead to cheeky grins,
While a slippery slope leads to cheeky spins.
Snowmen take selfies, their hats far too tall,
As they wink and wave, oh how they enthrall!

In the hush of the night, with snow banks so deep,
They share silly stories that never lose sleep.
With laughter that sparkles, like stars in their eyes,
Frosted fables linger, beneath chilly skies!

Whispers of Winter's Glow

Snowflakes dance on my nose,
As I trip on my own toes.
Hot cocoa spills on my coat,
Who knew this drink could float?

Elves are sneaking by the door,
Looking for snacks, not a chore.
Reindeer play tag on the roof,
Hope they don't drop a goof!

Jingle bells in a snowball fight,
Every laugh feels so right.
Sleighs are stuck in the drifts,
We take turns pushing, what a lift!

Gifts in trees, oh what a sight,
Wrapping paper takes flight.
With laughter and cheer we'll meet,
Winter's fun is such a treat!

Frosty Serenade at Midnight

The snowman sings off-key,
His carrot nose jumps with glee.
Froze my face and then my toes,
Brrr! Time to warm up, who knows?

Mittens twirling in the air,
While I laugh, without a care.
Hot cider spills on my pants,
Not the best for winter's dance!

The cat thinks snow is great fun,
Chasing flakes, oh what a run!
But now she's stuck in the snow,
Guess it's time for a warm glow!

Frosty friends gather near,
Sharing jokes and winter cheer.
With giggles lighting the night,
We find joy in every bite!

The Silent Night's Embrace

Whispers of snowflakes spin,
I snicker at the winter grin.
Frosted windows, sights so strange,
Where'd I leave my warm exchange?

Santa's sleigh is in a heap,
Turns out he got lost in sleep.
Reindeer nap by the fireplace,
Who knew they'd find this sweet place?

I'm wrapped up like a big burrito,
Trying to move, but I'm too slow.
Socks on the cat? What a scene!
She struts around like she's the queen!

With giggles echoing around,
Our laughter spreads without a sound.
In this frosty, funny place,
We find warmth in every space!

Starlit Dreams in December

Stars are shining, oh what fun,
Waiting for snow, everyone!
But I slip on the ice, whoa,
Guess I'm the star of the show!

Laughter floats on a chilly breeze,
While snowmen bend their knees.
Whipped cream fights in hot cocoa mugs,
Dodge the marshmallows and the hugs!

Tinsel tangled in my hair,
Decorations everywhere.
I'll dance like no one's here,
While neighbors watch and cheer!

The night is young, so let's play,
Build a snowman, come what may.
With excitement under the sky,
We laugh 'til we can't say goodbye!

The Silence of Falling Snowflakes

Snowflakes tumble, oh what a sight,
They whisper secrets on this silent night.
A snowman sneezes, then falls with a thud,
Head first in the yard, it turns into mud.

Listen closely, and you might hear,
A cheeky squirrel, drinking hot beer.
A snowball flies, right past my ear,
A moment's peace, till chaos is near!

Lights twinkle bright, like stars that bite,
And the cat thinks the tree is a flighty kite.
A dance of joy, around the cold,
With boots too big, and stories retold.

So let us revel in this frosty cheer,
With cocoa spills and laughter here.
As snowflakes fall, oh what a caper,
The winter nights are funny paper!

Peace Wrapped in Silver Light

In the glow of moonbeams, a cat takes a leap,
He lands on the table, and I spill my steep.
With feathers and fur as his Christmas gift,
He rolls on the tablecloth, gives it a lift.

Eggnog spills, and noses collide,
As we gather 'round, for the merry slide.
Uncle Joe dances, at least, he thinks so,
While Aunt Edna shouts, "You must do the dough!"

Mittens are lost, and socks are the prize,
As the puppy digs, with mischievous eyes.
Laughter erupts like the bubbles we chase,
In this silver light, there's warmth in the space.

Our toast to the season, let's make it a laugh,
For peace and good fortune, we need a good half.
In the glow of the moment, let good spirits reign,
We're all a bit foolish, but who'll cast the blame?

Béguinage of Frosty Serenades

In a world of frost, a choir takes stage,
With penguins and snowmen, they're filled with rage.
They honk like old geese, as they sing off-key,
While dancers in mittens trip over a bee.

Ice-skates are clumsy, like ducks in a row,
With giggles and slips, and a flurry of snow.
A jolly old fellow, who carries the cheer,
Trips over the tree, what a sight to revere!

Tinsel flies high, on playful dog tails,
As the carolers sing of wintery gales.
A frosty serenade, all in good jest,
Where laughter's the song, and joy's the best guest.

So let's strut our stuff in these frosty plays,
With snowball tosses that brighten our days.
With flapjack flops and jolly grand tunes,
We'll waltz 'neath the laughter of wintery moons!

Solstice Secrets Hidden in Twilight

In twilight's embrace, the cookies have fled,
The reindeer have nibbled, our snack cupboard's dead.
With sprinkles of chaos, and icing askew,
We bake festive cakes resembling a zoo.

Outside, all the kids wear hats far too big,
They tumble like bears, with hops and a jig.
As sleds turn to rockets, down hills they embark,
To crash in the bushes and laugh in the dark.

The secrets of solstice dance through the air,
With neighbors all grinning, running without care.
At midnight, we gather for laughter and cheer,
A toast with warm cider, to friends far and near!

So here's to the mishaps, the giggles, the fun,
The winter shenanigans, and snowball runs.
In shadows of twilight, let joy fill the space,
With secrets of laughter, our hearts now embrace!

Light's Dance Upon Winter's Veil

Twinkling bulbs atop a tree,
Cats are plotting, oh so slyly.
Ornaments bouncing with a cheer,
Santa's belly shakes, oh dear!

Snowmen frown, they've lost their hats,
Squirrels giggle, wearing spats.
Elves are tripping, it's a sight,
Candy canes causing delight!

Yule logs crackle, popcorn flies,
Grandma winks, amidst the pies.
A dance of light in frosty air,
Jingle bells ringing without a care!

Pine-scented dreams float on by,
Outside the reindeer leap and fly.
As laughter spills like winter's brew,
We'll sing, and dance, all night 'til blue!

Serenades of a Winter Evening

Snowflakes swirl, a glitzy fight,
Hot cocoa spills, much to delight.
Chubby cheeks with sticky hands,
Build a fort from snowman sands!

Socks are missing, where'd they go?
Grandpa's snoring steals the show.
Puppies dig in heaps of white,
Tails wag quick, what a sight!

Carolers croon with glee and style,
One forgets the words for a while.
They gather 'round with mugs in hand,
Sipping joy like it's unplanned!

With each laugh, the cold grows mild,
Merry chaos, again, we're wild.
Stories told by firelight's sway,
Winter magic in full display!

Ethereal Glow of the Longest Night

The moon's a pie with frosting bright,
    Rabbits dance in shiny light.
Sugar plums prance on candy canes,
While jolly spirits shake the chains!

Creaky doors, a squeaky toy,
    Santa plays with newfound joy.
Reindeer dodge 'neath mistletoe,
A peck on cheeks, hey, don't be slow!

Charming socks hung high and tight,
    Filled with treats, oh what a sight!
Laughter bubbles, like sparkling wine,
    Each giggle adds to the divine!

And when it's dawn, we'll all agree,
    That winter fun is pure esprit.
With snowball fights and frostbit toes,
    We'll kick up joy, let winter glow!

Celestial Ornaments in the Dark

Stars dangle low, like shiny beads,
Raccoons eye cookies, plotting feeds.
Snowflakes land on noses, oh!
Sprightly mischief, let it flow!

The tree's a tower of jumbled cheer,
Tinsel tangled, all draw near.
Wrapping paper flies through air,
Oops! I wrapped the cat, beware!

Jingle bells and hearty laughs,
Mom's lost her phone amidst the crafts.
Grandpa's hat flies off his head,
Into the punch? Now that's fed!

As laughter fades towards the night,
We gather 'round, warm hearts alight.
The spirit dances, cheeky and bright,
In every corner, pure delight!

Mistletoe Kisses and Twinkling Wishes

In the kitchen, cookies burn,
A cat is plotting its return.
Mistletoe's hung, the lights will twinkle,
But Uncle Joe's dance makes us all crinkle.

Grandma's fruitcake, quite the sight,
It wobbles like jelly, a funny fright.
A game of charades goes too far,
As cousin Sally pretends to be a star.

Snowflakes fall like clumsy fools,
Kids in their mittens, breaking all rules.
With laughter echoing through the night,
A snowman's hat flies, what a sight!

The punch bowl juggling turns to fun,
As someone spills, and we all run.
In this glow of laughter and cheer,
Who needs a silent night, my dear?

A Chill in the Air, a Warmth in the Heart

Jack Frost nips at our toes,
While Aunt Edna shows off her prose.
Squirrels invade the birdseed stash,
While Dad claims he can make a splash.

Hot cocoa spills down little Fred,
His jacket's now a marshmallow bed.
Mom's in her scarf, looking quite bold,
With a twinkle in her eye, never cold.

Outside, the snow makes a great slide,
While Dad's mid-joke, and we all hide.
His face turns red as he slips and slides,
While we all giggle, our joy won't hide.

But warmth fills the room, it's mild and bright,
With all our loved ones, it feels so right.
A chilly breeze can't steal this fun,
With laughter rings, we share as one.

Enchanted Snowflakes Falling

Snowflakes dance like tipsy sprites,
Landing on rooftops, giving frights.
The neighbors' lights blink out of sync,
And all we can do is laugh and think.

As snowmen rise with carrot nose,
Little Timmy trips, and down he goes.
Wrapped up snug in layers thick,
Fingers froze, but we still pick!

Whispers squeal with glee and gaffes,
As Grandma recounts her youthful laughs.
With every flake that drifts down low,
We build our laughter like a show.

A snowball fight erupts with zest,
And Aunt Sue claims she's the best.
In this world of chilly cheer,
We'll groove right through the frosty year.

Hushed Lullabies in December's Grip

The carolers sing off-key tonight,
While Dad believes he's quite the sight.
With jingle bells wrapped 'round his hat,
He prances about, a funny aristocrat.

Mom's making pies that wobble and shake,
While Fido's sneaking bites of the cake.
The oven beeps, the countdown's begun,
As cousin Jake tries to sneak and run.

The fireplace crackles and pops a tune,
And Aunt Liz twirls to the light of the moon.
In laughter we share, the silliness grows,
As Grandpa dozes and nobody knows.

The gift wrap's flying, it's a colorful fray,
And little ones giggle and play all day.
In a magic of laughter, cradled tight,
These lullabies rock us into the night.

The Magic of Twinkling Shadows

In the glow of lights so bright,
Elves dance silly, oh what a sight!
Snowflakes swirl, a sparkling show,
While dogs chase tails in the frosty glow.

Frosty breath in the chilly air,
Reindeer leap without a care!
Santa's list gets tangled tight,
As he giggles in pure delight.

Mittens lost and scarves gone rogue,
Snowmen giggle as they hedge a fog.
Hot cocoa spills on woolly socks,
While silly cats prance around in flocks.

The night is jolly, laughter rings,
With every jingle, happiness springs.
So grab a friend, let time stand still,
As shadows dance with mischievous thrill.

Enchanted Spirits in the Snow

Glimmers twinkle, the ghosts run wild,
Chasing each other, all beguiled.
Snowmen wobble, hats askew,
As giddy giggles rise anew.

Wishing wells freeze with hopes and dreams,
While prancing penguins slide in teams.
Frosty noses and cheeks so red,
Joyful chaos fills the night ahead.

Sleigh bells ring as the wind does blow,
Ghostly shivers in the muffled glow.
Cookies vanish, stealthy and sly,
As spirited snowflakes tumble by.

With every laugh upon the ground,
Whimsy tickles all around.
So join the fun, let spirits soar,
In frosty nights, there's so much more!

Celestial Secrets of December

Stars are winking with a playful gleam,
As snowflakes whisper secrets in a dream.
Sleds zoom past with chants of glee,
While snowballs fly, oh what a spree!

Twinkling lights on every tree,
Muffin tops and cocoa—oh, can it be?
Furry friends prance, socks on their paws,
Laughing loudly, they'll take a pause.

Pine trees sway, caught in the dance,
While kids in scarves take dreamy stance.
Jolly laughter fills the night,
With every inch of pure delight.

Under twinkling, enchanted skies,
Whimsy sparkles, oh how it flies!
So cozy up and share a grin,
As the magic of December begins.

Nocturnal Bliss Above Cozy Rooftops

Up on the rooftops, critters peek,
Silly antics make laughter leak.
Cats in hats take a festive stance,
Even the owls join the dance!

Beneath the stars, the giggles grow,
With elves who tumble in fresh snow.
Reindeer snack on cookies and fun,
Playful tricks are never done.

Light shines bright on frosty lanes,
While neighbors fight over snowball gains.
Merry mischief takes the night,
As everyone revels in pure delight.

So gather round with cheer and glee,
Under this sky, so warm and free.
In cozy nests, let laughter boom,
As the magic swirls in every room.

Radiance on Snow-Blanketed Streets

The snowflakes tumble, make a scene,
A snowman's hat looks too big, I mean!
Kids toss snowballs, giggles ensue,
But watch out, mom's laundry's in view!

Footprints lead to trouble galore,
Was that a penguin? Oh, it's a chore!
Sledding down hills, we zoom with glee,
But who knew the snowbank was so deep?

Hot chocolate spills, marshmallows fly,
A peppermint stick? It's a candy pie!
Laughter echoes, a joyful treat,
Even the dog gets caught on his feet!

With twinkling lights, the houses glow,
We wait for Santa while dancing in snow.
Who knew winter could bring such cheer?
Let's play again—next year, my dear!

Lullabies of Winter's Quiet Whisper

The frost nips sharply, don't lose your hat,
Everyone slips—oh wait, it's a cat!
Snowballs are flying, aim for the crew,
But it's Uncle Joe who ended up blue!

Icicles dangle, like teeth of a beast,
The car slides backward—what a feast!
Mom's baking cookies, a gingerbread dream,
But the dough that's left? It's not what it seems!

Sleds piled high, yet there's one no one chose,
The one with the hole—oh look at it go!
We giggle and snicker as we all race,
Adventures in snow, a wintertime chase!

As night draws close, we count all the stars,
And wonder if Santa will drive little cars.
With all this laughter and cocoa so warm,
The jingle of laughter is the heart's perfect charm!

A Tapestry of Frost and Light

The lights twinkle bright on the snowy ground,
A dog's made a snowman, what a sight—profound!
With carrots for noses and buttons galore,
It's a snow-laden party, who could want more?

All bundled up, we dash with delight,
But oh! Down the slide, what a funny flight!
Snowflakes fall gently, their delicate grace,
Yet one's stuck on dad's nose—oh what a face!

Snowball fights rage, laughter rings true,
The mom on the porch, she's in on it too!
Sleds zoom by, kids give their all,
Until someone bounces and crashes the wall!

As day turns to dusk, the frost starts to shine,
Carols and cookies, all warm and divine.
With chatter and giggles filling the air,
This winter's a blast, just nobody care!

Celestial Reflections in the Stillness

The stars above twinkle, so bright in the night,
As grandma dances, oh what a sight!
She's lost her shoe, slipped right on the ice,
But who can resist? It's just too nice!

Hot cider's bubbling, the recipes vary,
While children complain that no one will marry!
The carolers sing with their voices so grand,
But the cat's in the choir—mayhem at hand!

Frosty lamp posts look so full of cheer,
It's hard to be serious when friends are so near.
Santa's on break, his sleigh's in the shop,
But he'll still find us—just don't let it stop!

So gather around, with cocoa in sight,
We'll laugh through the night, till morning's delight.
Winter's a wonder, with joy and with fun,
Let's cherish this season as it's just begun!

Silver Shadows of a Sleeping World

In fluffy snow, the snowmen dance,
Their carrot noses in a silly prance,
Frosty hats askew in crazy style,
While mice take selfies, all in a pile.

The moon smirks down on joyful glee,
As cats glide past, all full of esprit,
Chasing squirrels in reindeer suits,
What a sight, oh, the winter loot!

Snowflakes twirl on a playful breeze,
Elves in shorts, caught teasing the freeze,
With snowball fights and giggles loud,
Each frosty laugh, makes winter proud.

So here's a toast to the merry night,
Where shadows shimmer, bathed in light,
With laughter ringing through the air,
Winter's whimsy, beyond compare.

Joyful Reflections in the Snow

Tiny reindeer, dressed so fine,
Practicing jumps, sipping elder wine,
Frosty friends, in silly hats,
Imitating well-fed chubby cats.

Snowballs fly with energetic cheer,
As snowmen giggle, downing a beer,
Their twiggy arms flail like rock stars,
Under the glow of shiny Mars.

Candy canes are up for a fight,
With peppermint sticks, oh what a sight!
Funky tunes from the frosty trees,
While penguins do a dance with ease.

Footprints lead to a hot cocoa stand,
Where snowflakes mingle, each one so grand,
Cheers ring out, hearts feeling bold,
In the land of winter, stories unfold.

Soft Lanterns Fading into Night

Glow worms chime with twinkling flair,
While gnomes juggle in the crisp night air,
A cat in boots leads the parade,
As sparkly lights begin to fade.

Whimsical laughter from rooftops high,
As snowflakes whistle and coyotes sigh,
The owls hoot, playing musical chairs,
As laughter echoes, floating in layers.

A festive squirrel steals a bulb,
Placing it right on a diva's skull,
With bright ideas and silly cheer,
Each moment draws the merry near.

So come, join the fun on this frosty eve,
With glowing lanterns, just believe,
In moments silly, slip and slide,
Under the stars where magic resides.

Carols Among the Pine Needles

Pine needles rustle like whispers low,
As critters gather for the holiday show,
Foxes in scarves sing in delight,
While owls join in, winging their flight.

The drums are banged by a bear so bold,
Toothbrush guitars strumming rock and roll,
With joyful rhythms, feet tap and slide,
As squirrels serve snacks, full of pride.

Around the tree with ornaments bright,
Critters spin tales by candlelight,
Nutmeg dreams and gingerbread tales,
Mixing with giggles and frosty gales.

So raise a cheer for this merry crew,
In the midst of the woods, full of fun for you,
Where carols are sung, laughter reigns,
In the heart of the pines, where joy remains.

Moonlight Waltz Among Pine Trees

Squirrels dance with twinkling lights,
Pine cones roll like snowball fights,
Elves lost trying to find their way,
A snowman dons a frosty beret.

Laughter rings from every bough,
Snowflakes falling, oh, what a plow!
Reindeer prance in silly parade,
Caught in a game of charades.

Bells jingle on the frosty air,
A raccoon borrowed grandma's chair,
Mischief brewed from the snowy night,
While tree ornaments take flight.

In shadowed glades, we spin and twirl,
As winter's chill makes laughter swirl,
Moonlit giggles fill the trees,
Where every branch is sure to tease.

Dreams Drenched in Winter's Haze

Snowmen dream of summer days,
Wishing for a sunbeam's rays,
While penguins on the ice do glide,
Riding sleds with glee and pride.

A warm mug slips from frozen hands,
Sending cocoa to snowy lands,
Chickens trying to take a flight,
Cluck in shades of holiday night.

Frosty foes in snowball fight,
Muffin pies in pure delight,
Pine trees swaying to a beat,
As carolers jump in their feet.

Giggles echo in the air,
While snowflakes catch in frozen hair,
Dreams may drift on winter's haze,
But joy remains in silly ways.

Glimmers of Hope in the Chill

Wreaths are hung with playful glee,
While cats watch from the festive tree,
Socks are stuffed with candy treats,
And choirs sing off pitch in beats.

A gingerbread man runs so fast,
With icing boots meant to outlast,
While cocoa spills with every cheer,
As sugar plums dance near the ear.

Fires crackle with jokes and puns,
While gumdrops race with peppermint runs,
A snowflake lands, what a surprise,
It's just a feather from grandma's pies!

In the chill, we toast and cheer,
For every moment brings us near,
Glimmers of joy, reflecting light,
In this whimsical, frosty night.

Nightfall's Embrace on a Festive Eve

Tinsel drops like starlit rain,
As reindeer tease a passing train,
Elves slip 'neath the mistletoe,
With dancing shoes and hearts aglow.

Cookies vanish, what a sight,
Crawling cats cause holiday fright,
The dog jumps high, his tail a blur,
In this festive, joyful stir.

Cardinals chirp their holiday tune,
While squirrels plan a nutty swoon,
Frosty cheeky winks at the moon,
Painting night with laughter's tune.

With every laugh, our hearts release,
As joy becomes a bubbly fleece,
Nightfall wraps us in delight,
While snowflakes dance till morning light.

The Spirit of Giving in the Frosty Air

Snowflakes dance, and socks await,
Gifts wrapped tight, with bows of fate.
Elves in the corner - all tied up,
Coffee cups spill like fudge-filled cup!

Reindeers prance on rooftops tall,
While Santa collides with a plastic wall.
Tinsel tangles in my hair,
Grandma's cookies, I just can't share!

Chilly cheeks and laughter flow,
Neighbors argue 'bout lights on show.
Mittens lost; oh what a quest,
Here's to the chaos; it's the best!

So raise your glass, take a good cheer,
For laughter is what brings us near.
Frosty air is full of zest,
Let silly joy be our true quest!

Twilight Hues in the Quiet Woods

Lights are twinkling, shadows fall,
Squirrels dart, they have a ball.
Snowmen wobble, hats askew,
Each carrot nose says, "What's new?"

Branches creak with secrets told,
Of mistletoe and stories bold.
Birds wrapped in scarves sing out loud,
While raccoons dance, all fluffy and proud.

Icicle chandeliers hang bright,
As woodland critters plan their night.
Every creature wears a grin,
While the bushes hide a giddy chin.

So gather 'round the glimmering trees,
Sip hot cocoa with a frosty breeze.
In cozy corners, joy takes flight,
As moonlit mischief claims the night!

Whispers of Frost-Kissed Nights

Frosty whispers float in air,
Woolly hats and pajamas rare.
Snowball fights between the pines,
Childlike laughter sings in lines.

The cat's caught in a Christmas light,
As dogs chase snowflakes in delight.
Pinecone turkeys on the lawn,
Who knew fun could be so drawn?

Chilly cheeks and rosy noses,
Hiding 'neath those prickly roses.
Grown-ups stuck in tinsel fights,
While kids giggle at the sights!

A night of joy and little pranks,
Furry friends give cozy thanks.
With winter's dance, we feel so free,
In this whimsy, just let it be!

Silver Lanterns in the Sky

Stars above in a jolly row,
Shiny lanterns swing and glow.
Some are upside down, it's true,
But that's the magic that ensues!

Hats that hover, mittens fly,
Silly snowmen give a sigh.
Through the snow, children yell,
"Look at me! I'm ringing bells!"

Chasing shadows 'neath the moon,
Sledding down to a winter tune.
Coal eyes wink and grin so wide,
"We spark fun, there's nothing to hide!"

Laughter echoing, heartbeats race,
Frosty breath leads the chase.
Let's make wishes, oh so bright,
For this wintery, merry night!

Milton Keynes UK
Ingram Content Group UK Ltd.
UKHW020046271124
451585UK00012B/1087